EHSAAS KE ALFAAZ

DIL SE KAAGAZ TAK

SARTHAK BHALLA

BookLeaf Publishing
India | USA | UK

Made with ❤ on the BookLeaf Publishing Platform
www.bookleafpub.in
www.bookleafpub.com

Dedication

इस किताब को उन एहसासों के नाम
जो कभी पूरी तरह कहे नहीं गए,
पर हर बार महसूस ज़रूर किए गए।
उन भावनाओं के नाम
जो शब्दों से पहले दिल में जन्म लेती हैं,
और कहे जाने से पहले ही
अपनी सच्चाई साबित कर देती हैं।
उन अनकहे जज़्बातों के लिए
जो हर इंसान के भीतर
चुपचाप अपना घर बना लेते हैं
बिना अनुमति,
बिना शोर।
To the silences that stayed,
to the emotions that waited for words,
and to the moments that quietly shaped who I became.
To the pauses between sentences,
where the real meaning often lived.
To the breaths I took
before admitting the truth to myself.
To the days that passed without milestones,
yet somehow changed me forever.

उन रातों के लिए जब मन बहुत कुछ कहना चाहता था,
पर शब्द साथ नहीं देते थे,
और ख़ामोशी ही सबसे सच्चा जवाब बन जाती थी।
उन रातों के लिए जब छत को ताकते हुए
ख़ुद से सवाल किए गए,
और जवाबों ने सुबह तक इंतज़ार किया।
जब नींद से ज़्यादा यादें भारी लगती थीं,
और दिल की आवाज़
सबसे तेज़ सुनाई देती थी।
And to the one
who arrived not as an answer,
but as a calm a pause, a presence, a feeling of home.
To the one who didn't fix anything,
yet somehow made everything lighter.
Who didn't promise forever,
but made the present feel enough.
Who taught me that comfort
can exist without explanations.
यह किताब न किसी शिकायत का बोझ है,
न किसी अधूरी कहानी का शोर।
यह उन पन्नों का संग्रह है
जहाँ दर्द भी सलीके से रखा गया है, और ख़ुशी को भी
बिना डर के जगह दी गई है।
जहाँ किसी को दोषी नहीं ठहराया गया,
सिवाय उस वक़्त के
जो समझने में लग गया।
जहाँ हर एहसास ईमानदारी से दर्ज हुआ है।

बिना सजावट, बिना नाटकीयता, बस वैसा ही
जैसा वह था।
मेरे कल के लिए,
जहाँ यह सब शुरू हुआ।
जहाँ पहली बार महसूस हुआ
कि महसूस करना ही
काफ़ी होता है।
मेरे आज के लिए,
जहाँ इन शब्दों ने आकार लिया।
जहाँ उलझनें भी स्वीकार हैं,
और ठहराव को
कमज़ोरी नहीं माना गया।
और उस आने वाले कल के लिए,
जिसे अब हम साथ लिखेंगे
बिना जल्दी के,
बिना साबित करने की ज़रूरत के।
धीरे, सच के साथ,
और पूरे दिल से।
क्योंकि यह किताब
ख़त्म होने के लिए नहीं लिखी गई
यह बस शुरू होने की
एक ईमानदार कोशिश है।

Preface

This book is not a confession. It is not an explanation.
It is simply a collection of feelings that found their way to paper.

यह उन एहसासों की यात्रा है
जो कभी दिल में रहे,
कभी शब्द बने,
और कभी बस ख़ामोशी में ही टिक गए।

Some pieces here are written in Hindi,
some in English.
Not by design,
but because emotions don't follow one language.

कुछ बातें
हिंदी में ही सच्ची लगती हैं, और कुछ
English ***में ही साँस ले पाती हैं।***

This book doesn't promise clarity.
It only offers honesty.

अगर इन पन्नों के बीच
आपको अपना कोई अनुभव,
कोई सवाल,
या कोई अधूरी-सी भावना
मिल जाए

then this book has done what it was meant to do.
These pages are not meant to be read in a hurry.

They ask for pauses.
For moments where you sit with a line
and let it sit with you.

यहाँ कोई निष्कर्ष नहीं है,
कोई सही या ग़लत का दावा नहीं।
यह केवल वह है
जो महसूस हुआ
और जैसा महसूस हुआ,
वैसा ही रहने दिया गया।

Some words may feel familiar,
some may feel uncomfortable.
Both reactions are welcome here.

यह किताब
किसी को समझाने के लिए नहीं लिखी गई,
बस साथ चलने के लिए लिखी गई है
बिना दिशा बताए,
बिना मंज़िल तय किए।

Read it where you feel safe.
Return to it when you need quiet.
And leave it open,
the way feelings often are.

Acknowledgements

This book exists because life happened

and because people stood beside me,

sometimes silently, sometimes firmly.

मैं सबसे पहले

अपने परिवार का आभार व्यक्त करता हूँ

To Maa,

whose care held me

long before I understood it.

Sanskruti Bhalla and Vasudha Dhanda,

my sisters, whose presence has always reminded

me

that home is not just a place,

but a feeling.

To Keshav Dhanda,

my brother

a quiet strength,

and a reminder that support doesn't always need

words.

To Kanika Ohri Bhalla, my wife
for being the calm I didn't know I was searching for.
For arriving not to change my past,
but to give it meaning.

This book may be written before us,
but it belongs to what we are building together.
And Shweta Arora,
my best friend
for listening without judgment,
for understanding without explanations,
and for standing by
even when words were still forming.
I am grateful to every experience
the gentle ones and the difficult ones
because both taught me how to feel honestly.

सबसे अधिक धन्यवाद
उस जीवन का
जिसने हर बार आसान रास्ता नहीं दिया,
पर हर बार, कुछ लिखने लायक ज़रूर दे गया।

If these pages manage to stay
with even one reader,
then this journey
has already been worth it.

1. अनजान बहुत है

अनजान बहुत है
ज़रा सी ज़िंदगी है,
अरमान बहुत है...
हमदर्द नहीं कोई,
इंसान बहुत है...

दिल का दर्द सुनाएँ तो
सुनाएँ किसको?
दिल के जो क़रीब हैं,
अनजान बहुत है...

धूप सी छलक जाए,
चाँदनी सा धोखा दे,
अपनों के ही शहर में,
महफ़ूज़ कौन है?

हर मोड़ पे मिलते हैं,
सपनों के सौदागर,
सच बोलने वालों से,
हैरान बहुत है...

छोटी सी ख़ुशबू भी,
अब महँगी लगती है,
दिल के बाज़ार में,
नुक़सान बहुत है...

ख़ामोशी के पन्नों पे,
लिखा है "सार" ने ये,
जो दर्द में साथ दे,
वो "मेहरबान" बहुत है...

ज़रा सी ज़िंदगी है,
और इम्तिहान बहुत है...

छुपी सी मुस्कानों में,
तूफ़ान बहुत है...
ज़रा सी ज़िंदगी है,
अरमान बहुत है...

हमदर्द नहीं कोई,
इंसान बहुत है...
दिल का दर्द सुनाएँ तो
सुनाएँ किसको?
दिल के जो क़रीब हैं,
अनजान बहुत है...

2. Favourite Poem

Shall we, for once,
read my favourite poem slow,
side by side,
letting every quiet word we know
lead you gently back to me
like verses finding rhyme,
like pauses learning
how to wait for time.

Will you still call me
by my given name,
like an old friend does,
soft, unchanged?
Or tease me lightly
with the worlds I love,
fictional lives
I still believe in enough.

Will you return to it
once, then twice,
then stay a little longer than advised?
Read it again,
and then again,
until "last time"
forgets to end.

Or will you leave me here
with the night at three,
unfinished thoughts
keeping company?
Loose lines, half-feelings,
no full stop
just a heart
that doesn't know when to stop.

Either way,
you remain the same
you are that poem
I never outgrew or renamed.
That one line
that hooks my breath,
pulls me back
with quiet depth.

I trace you slowly

with careful hands,
re-read you till
the pages can't stand.
The words begin to blur,
yet I refuse to turn
some endings
don't need to be learned.

And somewhere
between silence and sense,
when meaning finally drops its defence,
"Saar" writes this truth—
steady, alone:

You don't stay a memory, overgrown—
you become the poem
I keep coming home to,
alone.

3. कौन?

मैं रूठूँ तो,
तुम भी रूठ जाओ,
तो मनाएगा कौन?

कल जो अपने थे,
उन अपनों को
समझाएगा कौन?

दिल के कोने में
बैठी है एक ख़ामोशी-सी,
पर इस ख़ामोशी को
शोर बनाएगा कौन?

यादों के टुकड़ों को
कैसे जोड़ पाएँगे,
जो टूट गया है,
उस डोर को
बाँधेगा कौन?

ज़िद्दों के सफ़र में
खो गया है प्यार कहीं,
फिर इस सफ़र से
वापस लौट आएगा कौन?

रिश्ता बनाकर
तोड़ते रहना
तो आसान है,
पर हर बार
तोड़ के
फिर से बनाएगा कौन?

आज अगर है साथ
तो एहसास कर ले,
कल ख़ाली हाथों को
पकड़ेगा कौन?

मैं चुप,
तुम भी चुप,
फिर इस चुप्पी को
"सार" तोड़ेगा कौन?
छोटी-छोटी बातों को
दिल से लगा लोगे,
फिर रिश्ता
निभाएगा कौन?

ना मैं राज़ी,
ना तुम राज़ी,
फिर माफ़ करेगा कौन?

ज़िंदगी नहीं मिलती
हमेशा के लिए,
कल को कोई
एक ना रहा,
फिर पछताएगा कौन?

ज़िंदगी
एक दफ़ा का तोहफ़ा है,
पर इस तोहफ़े की
क़दर कराएगा कौन?

4. A Letter in Case I Forget

Fears, as such
everything drifts in a daze.
What if I wake up one day
and forget your face?

What if I forget the way
you held my hand tight,
or the soft, final kiss
before saying goodnight?

What if I forget all the walks we took,
yet still remember the lanes
the silent roads
that learned our names?

What if I forget your scent,
the one that stayed on your tees,
folded away in my cupboard,
clinging quietly to me?

What if I wake up one day
with nothing left to say?
No words waiting,
no reasons to stay?

What if I wake up
and forget our home's quiet art
those corners where memories
learned how to stay in the dark?

And what if I forget the moments
I lived only with you,
the last fragile pieces
of what we once knew?

Maybe one day
I'll wake without fear,
without these nights
that keep you near.

Maybe one day
the memories will fade,
my heart and my head
clear in daylight.

And if our paths ever cross again,
through time, through chance, through you

I know this much:
I would still choose you.

Somewhere between fear and forgetting,
"Saar" leaves this truth
you will always exist
in my version of you.

And if not,
I hope this letter
does what I couldn't do
stand in your silence
and remind you of me, too

5. तू चाहिए

काश मेरी ज़िंदगी का हर फ़ैसला
तुमसे जुड़े,
हर राह तुम तक आए,
हर मोड़ तुम पर रुके।

मेरी बाहों में छुप जाए
हर ग़म का असर,
बस तेरा प्यार मिले
और ना हो कोई ख़बर।

तेरी आँखों के जहाँ में
बस डूबता रहूँ,
तेरे लबों के सुरों में
ही मैं खो जाऊँ।

मेरी हर धड़कन का
मक़सद तू बन जाए,
और दुनिया से परे
एक नई दास्तान बन जाए।

मेरे सपनों के शहर में
बस तेरा उजाला हो,
तेरा साथ हो,
बस ये हर दिन का हवाले हो।

तेरे होने से ही
ज़िंदगी पूरी लगे,
तेरी ख़ुशी
मेरी दुआ का नूर बन के जगे।

इन ख़्वाहिशों के बीच
"सार" बस इतना लिख पाए

काश तुम पूछो मुझसे
क्या चाहिए,
मैं पकड़ूँ हाथ तेरा
और कहूँ

तेरा साथ चाहिए।
मेरी आँखों के सामने
तू मुस्कुराती हुई
हमेशा चाहिए।

6. It's You

It's you.
The one I want to come home to,
after days that drain me through and through.

The one I roll toward in the quiet of night,
wake up beside,
morning after morning,

when everything feels right.
It's you I want on late-night runs,
for food, for air, for stupid fun,
just to escape these silent rooms,
just to feel close, just to move.

The one for little dates and candlelight,
movies, dinners,
soft-spoken nights.

And longer days that lose their way
drives with no end,

parks, gardens,
time that forgets the date.

It's you I want for reckless plans,
lakes, long walks, holding hands,
woods that listen, streets that sleep,
moments the world agrees to keep.

It's you I want to stay in for,
build small forts on the living-room floor,
movies playing, worries gone,
favourite food till the night feels warm.

And somewhere between these simple truths,
"Saar" learns what choosing you can do

it isn't places,
or things we start,
it's you,
every time,
my heart.

I want to make you smile for life,
hold you closer when days are tight.
Be the calm when your world breaks down,
be the one who stays around.

All my good days,
all my bad,
every version of the life I have
I want them with you,
through and through.
It's you.

It's always been you.
I swear I've never known this kind of truth,
never stood this sure, this rooted, this true.

No doubt, no fear, no second view
it's you.

7. इश्क़ के इम्तिहान

मोहब्बत की दास्तान में अक्सर
डूबते हैं लोग,
कभी नज़र में,
तो कभी तन्हाई में
टूटते हैं लोग।

प्यार में लोगों को
गिरते–संभलते
देखा है मैंने,

कोई चुपके से रोया,
तो किसी को
ख़ामोश होते
देखा है मैंने।

इश्क़ में डूबे दिलों को
ताक़त की ढाल में भी
कमज़ोर बनते
देखा है मैंने,

इस जुनून में
हदें पार होती
देखी हैं मैंने।
किसी को रूठते,

और किसी को
अंदर ही अंदर
मरते
देखा है मैंने।

कितना अजीब
इम्तिहान है ये इश्क़ भी
साथ रहने में दर्द,
और दूर जाने में भी
तकलीफ़ सहते,
"सार !!" बनते
देखा है मैंने।

तसव्वुर और तस्वीर के
बीच का फ़र्क़
होते
देखा है मैंने,

इश्क़ और तन्हाइयों के
फ़ासलों को
नापते दिल
देखे हैं मैंने।

सुकून की तलाश में
रूहों को भटकते
देखा है मैंने,

और इन लफ़्ज़ों के जुनून में
ख़ुद को महफ़ूज़ होते
देखा है मैंने।

8. Of Time, Travel, and Throwbacks

Take me back,
to a softer time,
when your confusion
somehow felt like mine.

Take me back,
to those fragile days,
when your silence
still knew my ways.

Take me back,
to the nights I knew,
how to colour my sky
in the shade of you.

When every blue
meant hope, not ache,
and every dawn
was yours to take.

Take me back,
to when my mind
painted futures
where we were aligned.

When every thought
ended in us,
and doubt felt distant,
small, unjust.

Take me back,
to the dusk-lit air,
when I waited for you
without despair.

I longed for you
as the sun went low,
while you were busy
counting stars I didn't know.

Take me back,
to that naïve art,
of holding on
with an open heart.

When I just waited,

steady, still,
and you just left
by choice, not will.

Somewhere between
memory and ache,
"Saar" pauses
and learns what time won't remake.

That not every past
is meant to stay,
some are lessons
that fade away.

So take me back,
just for a view,
not to stay
just to remember you.

Or maybe not.
Maybe let it be.
Some doors look kinder
when they stay in memory.

9. गोद

मिट्टी की खुशबू, घुटनों पे धूल,
काग़ज़ की नावें, सपनों का स्कूल।
माँ की हँसी—घंटी-सी बजे,
लोरी में चाँद, नींद से सजे।

कभी टूटे खिलौने, आँसू का शोर,
माँ बोले—"अरे, हो गया अब छोड़।"
रोटी में प्यार, दूध में कहानी,
हर डर का इलाज—माँ की जुबानी।

फिर कंधों पे बस्ता, आँखों में आग,
दौड़ते दिन, आगे बढ़ने की चाह।
कभी हँसी ठहाके, कभी ज़िद की बात,
छुप-छुप कर रोना—पहली-सी रात।

आईने में चेहरा, बदली-सी चाल,
दिल में शरारत, माथे पे सवाल।
माँ हँस के बोले—"समय भी अजीब,"
मैं समझा नहीं, पर लगा कुछ क़रीब।

अब शब्द सधे हैं, बोझिल-सा दिन,
हँसी भी निभानी पड़ती है हर दिन।
काम की गिनती, रिश्तों की रीत,
दिल का बचपन रह गया, अधूरी-सी जीत।

कभी राह में ठोकर, कभी मन बेहाल,
लौटा जब टूटकर—माँ ही बनी ढाल।
बिना पूछे समझे, बिना बोले थामे,
मेरे हर टूटे वाक्य—उसने ख़ामोशी में संभाले।

आज जो हूँ, उसमें उसकी धूप है,
मेरी हर छाया में माँ का रूप है।
और अगर कहीं फिर मिलना तय हो,
तो बस इतना-सा लिख दूँ दुआ की लकीर में

मांग लूं यह मन्नत की फिर यही जहाँ मिले,
फिर वही गोद फिर वही माँ मिले !!!

"सार" कहे—चलते-चलते समझ आई एक बात,
जग ने बहुत कुछ दे दिया, माँ ने दी औक़ात।
जहाँ सब रिश्ते तौल लिए, वहाँ भी कुछ कम था,
माँ की गोद न होती अगर, तो सब कुछ भ्रम था।

10. The Blanket I Found Again

I was eight years old,
and sleep came slow,
without my favourite blanket
I just couldn't let go.

I cried when they washed it,
waited up all night,
it kept me safe
till the morning light.

Safe from the monsters
under my bed,
from the shadow by the window
that lived in my head.

Later I learned
those ghosts weren't real
just branches of a tree
and the dark's quiet feel.

That blanket felt magic,
a soft little space,
where dreams were kept safe
and returned to their place.

I'd fold myself in
and drift far away,
saving my dreams
for another night's play.

Under its warmth
I could be anyone
a hero, an astronaut,
chasing the sun.

All the bedtime stories
my mother would say
turned into worlds
where I wanted to stay.

Wrapped in that cloth
I wasn't shy or small,
I fought fire-breathing dragons
and answered the call.

I wasn't alone,
not even at night
the blanket and dreams
held me just right.

And then I met you,
and quietly knew
that feeling returned,
old and true.

The same gentle warmth,
the same steady calm
"Saar" calls it now
what it always was:
you!!!.

11. सपनों ने आज नंगे पाँव चलना सीखा है

सपनों ने आज नंगे पाँव चलना सीखा है,
चुपके-चुपके आँखों में ढलना सीखा है।

पलकों की गलियों में हँसते-हँसते आए,
नींद के संग मिलकर मीठे गीत सुनाए।

चाँद ने आज लोरी गुनगुनाई है,
तारों ने तकिये पर रोशनी बिछाई है।

डर को सुलाया, शोर को सिखाया
धीरे बोलो, आज सपना प्यारा सा आया।

खिड़की के बाहर पेड़ भी झूम गए हैं,
हवा ने परियों के किस्से चुन लिए हैं।

बादल ने ओढ़ी रुई-सी चादर,
रात ने थाम लिया नन्हा-सा सफ़र।

खिलौने फुसफुसाए—"अब सो जाओ,"
कल फिर खेलेंगे, सपने सजाओ।

झपकी आई, पलकों ने गुनगुनाया,
नींद ने माथे पर प्यार चढ़ाया।

"सार" भी धीरे से यही समझाए,
अब तो सोने का पल आ जाए।

आँखें मींचो, सपनों को बुलाओ—
नींद की बाहों में खो जाओ।

12. For Women, Unseen and Unbowed

She wears her strength like borrowed light,
smiles bravely through the longest nights.

By day she laughs, she holds her ground,
by night her fears come circling round.

They see the mask, they praise the face,
never the cracks she learns to lace.

The world believes she's made of stone,
but strength feels heavy when alone.

They call her wise, the one who knows,
the one who fixes others' woes.

She gives, she listens, never breaks
at least, that's what the daylight takes.

Yet fears walk home with her each day,
lie beside dreams that drift away.

They make her feel so small, so thin,
as if the war lives under skin.

Still she stays. Still she tries.
Still hope glimmers in tired eyes.

Strong not because she never fell,
but because she rose and lived to tell.

"Saar" knows this truth, steady and clear:
your strength is real, never doubt it, dear.

13. रंगहीन आईना

इश्क़ की आँखों में रंगों की कमी क्या थी,
फिर भी हँसती तस्वीर को स्याह-सफ़ेद बनाया गया...

न रौशनी का नूर था, न साए का असर,
बस एक ख़ामोश लम्हा था जो चेहरे पे सजाया गया।

दिलों के राज़ थे, आँखों के अश्क़ में छुप गए,
स्याह-सफ़ेद तस्वीर में जज़्बात भी धुँधलाया गया...

उस मुस्कान में थी कहानियों की किताब पूरी,
मगर हर लफ़्ज़ को ख़ुद ही से छुपाया गया।

लबों तक आई बात भी साँसों में ठहर गई,
हर एक एहसास को आदत-सी सिखाई गई।

जो कहना था, वो निगाहों ने ही कह दिया,
और बोलने से पहले ही आवाज़ दबाई गई।

रंग होते हुए भी आँखों ने सादगी चुनी,
भीड़ में रहकर भी तन्हाई को ही बुनी।

हर धड़कन में था इक नाम अनकहा-सा,
मगर हर ख़्वाहिश ख़ुद से ही रूठी रही।

वक़्त ने रंग माँगे, हमने चुप्पी ओढ़ ली,
हर चाहत को तह-ए-दिल में ही दबाया गया।

जो कहा नहीं गया, वही सबसे गहरा रहा,
और उसी ख़ामोशी को पहचान बनाया गया।

"सार " कहता है, तस्वीर स्याह-सफ़ेद ही सही,
पर दिल की तह में इश्क़ पूरा बसाया गया।

जो दिखा नहीं दुनिया को, वही सच था शायद,
बस नज़र से नहीं, रूह से निभाया गया।

14. Weekend Love

What am I, but your weekend love,
A borrowed sky, a passing dove?

What is love to you, I ask
A skipped-beat song, you never play?

I dream in depths, I feel in flame,
I charm, they say, but hide my pain.

For every smile the world can see,
There's "Saar" alone inside of me

The one who walks when crowds depart,
Who learns his name by breaking heart.
I roam through streets unpolished, bare,
Through foreign winds, unfamiliar air,

In search of her no grand design,
Just peace in heart, just soul in line.
She's by a lake where silence sings,

Where water knows unhurried things,

Close to earth, to breath, to grace,
Far from noise, near nature's face.
She's not rare don't get me wrong,
She's not a verse too hard or long.

She's someone who would always say
"I love you" in the smallest way.
She'd feel the joy in others' cheer,
Sit with loss, stay with fear.

Lean on my shoulder, hum a tune,
Sing at dusk or random noon.
She'd hate my coffee, love me still,
Argue softly, stubborn will.

Teach me dance no eyes, no shame,
Turn awkward steps to playful flame.
A poet's heart, romance her art,
Believes in giving, not in part.

She's not an exception, not divine
Just not the one meant to be mine.
Like lashes wished in falling flight,
One storm-lit, fractured, wild night,

When skies wore sun and moon in seam,
I found you like a broken dream.
You held my hand as forests pulled,
As storms grew loud and darkness full.

My search for love felt briefly done
When rain and body both begun.
You were gentle, soft, unclear,
A kindness blurred by falling fear.

My glasses fogged, the world went slow,
Despair rained hard I didn't know.
Next day, a letter dressed in grace,
Romancing time, each second, place.

"My hand," you wrote, "felt feather-light,
Like pigeon plumes in drifting flight."
You sent a flower rare, they say,
Blooms once a year, then fades away.

"Rare and beautiful," were your words,
I heard us never heard the verbs.
We rode the wheel, the world stood still,
You kissed me high above free will.

You were the moon I'd loved afar,
Now close enough to bruise a star.

Was it the height or lips that shook?
I still don't know which breath I took.

An old-town theatre, dusty screen,
A love story from the '90s scene.
I said, "It breaks me ,love denied
By caste and coin and social pride."

You smiled slow, as if you knew,
And said one word "Empathy," too.
I took you where the river ends,
Where city noise no longer bends.

We dipped our toes, carved stone with tale,
Let time grow tired, let stars prevail.
We counted lights as day withdrew,
I wished for "forever,"
You smiled "me too."

"Let's whisper wishes to the moon,"
You said beneath a silver noon.
It felt like fate, a perfect art
My fairytale, my foolish heart.

Till you left no sound, no clue,
No last page signed, no farewell view.
I searched the streets, I searched my head,

You weren't alive, you weren't dead.

In memory, you smiled again,
And named my ache "Longing," then.
You defined each word we'd share,
Each feeling folded in your care.

You made me trust the word "always,"
You taught my hope its shortest days.
"My hand's a feather," you once said
I missed the part where it would shred.

You called the flower rare and true,
I thought you meant us
You meant you.

Trust blooms short in modern time,
Loyalty's a fading rhyme.
learned too late what kindness means,
When it was mine, but never seen.

When you said, "Wish upon the moon,"
Did you already know how soon
She'd be the only one I'd trust
Once you were gone, reduced to dust?

Some truths are sharp, best left unsaid,

Your reason sleeps with words long dead.
You left regardless clean, complete,
Left "Saar" with storms and aching feet.

What am I now, but leftover rain,
Waiting for woods to pull me again?

What am I, but your weekend love
A borrowed sky, a passing dove?
What is love to you, it seems
A skipped-beat song,
You never play.

15. प्रेम

प्रेम पूछे तो कहना उससे
यह माँग नहीं, यह दान हुआ,
जो सौदा लगे संसार को,
वह भक्ति में भगवान हुआ।

सब कहते हैं प्रेम पा लेना,
कोई यह नहीं समझाया
जिसे पाने की चाह जगे,
वह प्रेम नहीं कहलाया।

यह कथा प्रेम सिखाने की है,
न पाने की, न जताने की,
जहाँ भाव स्वयं गुरु बन जाए,
और प्रेम हो सीख निभाने की।

प्रेम जब समझ में आने लगा,
तो मीरा का नाम उभरा,
जिसे पाने की चाह न थी उसमें,
बस देने का अर्थ निखरा।

उसने प्रेम किया था श्याम से,
पर अधिकार का भार न लिया,
जिसे जग ने सौदा समझा था,
उसे उसने समर्पण किया।

राधा ने प्रेम को मौन रखा,
अधिकारों से दूर निभाया,
जो पास रहकर भी दूर रहे,
उसी ने कान्हा को पाया।

राम ने प्रेम निभाया वन में,
राज नहीं, वचन चुना,
सीता ने प्रेम जिया धैर्य में,
जहाँ त्याग ही भूषण बना।

न वहाँ रास, न बाँसुरी थी,
न शब्दों का कोई विस्तार,
फिर भी प्रेम मर्यादा बनकर,
आज भी देता है आकार।

गोपियाँ आईं, रास रचा,
क्षण भर में रंग सजाया,
हँसी, स्पर्श, और क्षणिक चाह
पर प्रेम को बाँध न पाया।

सुदामा आया रिक्त हाथ,
न कुछ माँगा, न कुछ जताया,

मित्रता में जो झुका नहीं,
उसी ने राज कमाया।

द्रौपदी ने जब पुकारा श्याम,
न शब्द, न विधि अपनाया,
बस विश्वास को थामा उसने,
और प्रेम ने वस्त्र बन पाया।

मीरा ने यह सब देख लिया,
और एक ही पथ अपनाया
जो माँग बने, वह प्रेम नहीं,
जो छूट सके, वही निभाया।

कान्हा ने हर रिश्ते में,
एक ही सत्य दोहराया
प्रेम अधिकार नहीं होता,
वह केवल अर्पण सिखलाया।

और यही उस प्रेम का "सार" हुआ
जो तृष्णा नहीं, विश्वास हुआ,
जो पाया नहीं, पर पूर्ण रहा,
जो छूकर नहीं, साँस हुआ।

16. Painting My Own Skies

I spent my years learning how to stay,
Reading rooms, bending light my way.
I borrowed weather, softened tone,
Afraid to stand in skies my own.

I waited for signs disguised as fate,
Called delay wisdom, silence strength.
I shrank my needs, I softened blue,
And named it love as I withdrew.

I learned to smile at half-felt days,
To dress my wounds in fading grace.
I folded truth, adjusted size,
To fit inside accepted lives.

I stayed where effort paid the cost,
Where being seen felt nearly lost.
I told myself this was the test,
That quiet hearts are always blessed.

I carried dreams I never chose,
Wore wayward clouds like borrowed clothes.
I stood in storms not meant for me,
Calling endurance dignity.

Nothing shattered, no loud goodbye,
Just a slow ache behind the eyes.
Some truths don't scream, don't break, don't cry,
They wait till you're too tired to lie.

I saw how often I stepped aside,
How often I dimmed my inner sky.
I wasn't weak, just not yet free,
Still living life second-handedly.

And there, at last, I learned "Saar"
No one else defines who you are.
Healing begins the day you realise
Your life asks courage, not alibis.

Because sometimes it takes forever to realise
why it mattered, why it was wise
to stop waiting on borrowed skies,
and finally learn
to paint your own skies.

17. निर्वाह

हँसी पहनी, डर छुपाया,
दिन काटे, सच जलाया।

भीड़ मिली, मन वीरान,
शोर बहुत, भीतर सन्नाटान।

काम चला, दिल रुका,
नाम बढ़ा, इंसान झुका।

नींद टली, ख़्वाब दबे,
जागे तन, जज़्बात सड़े।

दर्द कहा, "ये दौर है",
रोज़ टूटना अब शौर है।

आँसू माने कमज़ोरी,
संभलना सीखा मजबूरी।

सच बोझा, झूठ सहारा,
भीतर बच्चा सबसे हारा।

वक़्त बिका, साँसें उधार,
जीवन बना बस कारोबार।

प्यार मिला, डर में लिपटा,
पास रहा, दिल में सिमटा।

दिल थका, होंठ सिले,
सोच चली, सौदे गिने।

रिश्ते तौले, मोल लगे,
कम माँगा, ज़्यादा सहे।

साथ रहे, पर दूर रहे,
डर था—कहीं सच न कहें।

वादा हल्का, छोड़ना सरल,
निभाना आज सबसे कठिन पल।

रुकना पाप, चलना रीत,
थकना माना हार की जीत।

ख़ुद से मिलना टलता गया,
आईना भी खलता गया।

डर को कहा "समय की चाल",
भागने को दी "समझ की ढाल।"

हर सवाल बना असहज,
हर मौन हुआ सामाजिक सहज।

धीरे-धीरे सब सीखा,
कैसे ज़िंदा रहकर फीका।

मौत नहीं, ये रोज़ की मार,
चलती साँस, सूना संसार।

और अंत में
"सार" कहे

"सुन रे जीव,
भाव बिना क्या जीवन जीव?
डर में जीया, मौन ओढ़ा,
साँस चली, पर जीवन छोड़ा।"

18. Not Tonight

The room was dim, not dark enough,
A single bulb hung tired and rough.
Walls held breaths they couldn't keep,
Time leaned heavy, refused to sleep.

Rain tapped softly on the pane,
Like second thoughts that ache in rain.
A chair stood still, a clock stood loud,
Silence dressed itself in sound.

On the table paper, plain,
Folded once, then folded pain.
No scent of hope, no spark of flame,
Just quiet words that asked no name.

This was not love.
Not loss.
Not war.
It was the pause before the door.

A silent cry, a distant dream,
A devil's smile half-truth, half-mean.
I stood between what life had taught
And what my heart still loosely sought.

They said all dreams burn fast and bright,
Ash by dawn, gone by night.
So I learned to choke my pleas,
Build worlds from my own miseries.

A nightmare learned my breathing well,
Knew which thought would ring the bell.
I searched for exits, cursed the sky,
Watched melted wings go drifting by.

Like Icarus, I feared the height,
Not of the fall but daring flight.
Not sun, not sea, not gods above
Just what might happen if I loved.

Too afraid to love, too afraid to die,
Too scared to stay, too tired to try.
A shallow man in oceans wide,
Drowning slow, with arms tied tight.

That letter waited thin and still,
A folded truth against my will.

I feared its ink could name my worth,
Or end the small hope I'd rehearsed.

What if distance sharpened each line?
What if "us" had run out of time?
What if you found someone complete,
And I was just a passing street?

I hadn't written, hadn't dared,
Silence felt safer than being spared.
So I told myself, not tonight,
Fear dressed patience as insight.

I'll leave it closed, let hours pass,
Let courage form or slowly crack.
Maybe you'll come, ask why I stayed,
Why I never wrote back, never prayed.

Maybe you'll read it slow, aloud,
Not like judgment, not too proud.
And maybe hope will sit nearby,
Not asking more just asking why.

And here, "Saar" learns the quiet art:
Fear isn't depth it's just the start.
For love demands one simple truth
You don't stay safe by staying mute.

Some letters aren't meant to wait,
They age into regret and fate.
And life doesn't end when truth appears
It ends when we let fear steer years.

So if hope knocks don't dim the light.
Don't wait to love.
Don't wait to die.

19. एक कप चाय के बाद

झील के किनारे

झील के किनारे बैठा हूँ, शाम ठहरी हुई,
पानी पर काँपती रौशनी कुछ कहती हुई।
हवा धीमे-धीमे पन्ने पलटती जाती है,
मेरी क़लम हर लहर के साथ तुम्हें लिख आती है।

इस सन्नाटे में तुम ख़याल बनकर आती हो,
बिना आवाज़ किए पूरा माहौल भर जाती हो।
कद में ठहराव, चाल में कोई जल्दबाज़ी नहीं,
जैसे हर क़दम जानता हो दिखावे की ज़रूरत नहीं।

चेहरा न बहुत सजा, न बिल्कुल सादा,
बस वही निखार जो शाम को भी कर दे आधा।
आँखों में सजावट नहीं, असर बोलता है,
एक नज़र काफ़ी है बाक़ी सब थम जाता है।

होंठों पर रंग हल्का, मुस्कान सधी हुई,
जैसे हर बात पहले सोची, फिर कही हुई।

माथे के बीच वो काली-सी बिंदी सजी हुई,
जैसे हर नज़र की मंज़िल वहीं आकर थमी हुई।

साड़ी जब पहनती हो, बात बदल जाती है,
हर नज़र बिना पूछे ठहर जाती है।
रंग वो नहीं जो चिल्लाकर दिखाया जाए,
बस इतना कि शाम भी खुद को दोहराए।

पल्लू ज़रा-सा हिलता है साँसों के साथ,
जैसे कोई राज़ रखा हो बहुत पास।
न कसाव, न ढील बस एक सधी हुई चाल,
जिसमें औरत नहीं, पूरी आदत बन जाए ख़याल।

इसी लय में चाय का ख़याल उतर आता है,
भाप के संग-संग मन भी मुस्कुराता है।
मैं लिखते-लिखते ठहर जाता हूँ इसी बात पर,
कि शायद पहली मुलाक़ात
यहीं से शुरू हो जाती है अक्सर।

चाय

चाय का ख़याल आते ही शाम मुस्काती है,
झील की लहर भी जैसे थोड़ा पास आती है।
कप की गरमी हथेलियों में उतर जाती है,
और मन की थकान, धीरे-धीरे छूट जाती है।

कभी ख़यालों में आए हो तुम,
कभी ख़ुशबू बन के छाए हो तुम।
हर पल में इक नर्मी थी,
जैसे शाम के बाद की चाय हो तुम।

बातें तुम्हारी नर्म-सी लगतीं,
मुस्कान में थोड़ी मिठास छुपी होती।
निगाहें तो जैसे अदरक-सी,
थोड़ा तेज़ , पर लज़्ज़त भरी होती।

फ़ुर्सत मिले तो आएँगे और पिएँगे,
एक कप हम भी...
सुना है तुम चाय में इलायची
मुँह से तोड़कर डालती हो...

यहीं से, शाम कुछ आगे बढ़ जाती है,
चाय ख़त्म नहीं होती
बस मुलाक़ात की संभावना
पास आती है।

कहने से पहले

शाम उसी झील के पास थमी रहती है,
जहाँ हर बात बिना कहे कही रहती है।

रोशनी हल्की-सी, हवा सधी हुई,
और वक़्त भी आज धीरे-धीरे
हमारा साथ निभाती है।

तुम सामने बैठी हो, बात अपने आप चलती है,
कोई बनावट नहीं, बस सादगी पलती है।
तुम्हारा यूँ देखना, फिर नज़र झुका लेना,
हर छोटी-सी अदा
दिल में जगह बना लेती है।

मैं कुछ कहता नहीं, फिर भी बहुत कुछ होता है,
तुम चुप हो, और वही
सबसे साफ़ लगता है।
इस एक शाम में
इतना कुछ समा जाता है,
कि सवाल अपने आप
आस-पास आ जाता है।

अटकता हुआ जवाब

मैं तुम्हें देखता हूँ, और क़लम रुक जाती है,
जो लिखना था दिल में, वही बात बन जाती है।
लफ़्ज़ सधे रहते हैं, आवाज़ भी धीमी,
पर उस खामोशी में भी बात पूरी कही जाती है।

मैं पूछता हूँ कुछ यूँ, बिना कोई दावा किए,
ना वादों की गठरी, ना सपनों के साये लिए।
"अगर ये पल, ये ठहराव, तुम्हें अपना लगे,
तो क्या इस एहसास को उम्र भर की आदत लिखें?"

इतना कहते ही आसमान गरज पड़ता है,
पहली बूँद झील को छूकर कहानी बदलता है।
बारिश अचानक हर आवाज़ ढक लेती है,
और जवाब...
हवा में कहीं अटक जाता है।

मैं फिर से क़लम उठाता हूँ, वही किनारा, वही पानी,
तुम्हारा नाम आधी पंक्ति, आधी कहानी।

जो बचा है इस ख़ामोशी के बाद वही है "सार",
अब पाठक तय करे,
उस बारिश में
हाँ था...
या फिर
इंतज़ार।

20. At The End

Maybe sooner than we think,
maybe closer than we know,
there's a turn we haven't taken,
a quiet, waiting "so."
What if this breath is the moment,
not a draft, not a rehearsal bit
no later scene, no second take
what if this is it?

I've learned the truest thing about life
wears the name we try to flee.
Everything else feels temporary,
borrowed faith, polite deceit.
Dreams expire, people change,
even love can lose its fit
but death alone stays constant,
undeniable, definite.

Words are bullets more than bridges,
said too fast, then left to sting.

People turn into the hollow
where unspoken endings sink.
Ships don't drown because of oceans,
they sink from cracks within
and death just watches quietly,
never pushing, never in.

We curse it like it's stealing,
as if something went unfairly wrong,
as if life promised permanence
and death didn't belong.
But death takes nothing personal,
it doesn't bargain, ask, or plead

it only rings the morning bell
and says, wake up and choose your speed.
It's an alarm without a snooze,
a truth that never needs disguise.
No reward waits on the other side,
no debt, no excuses left to hide.

You can't outrun it, can't outsmart it,
can't make it quit
you can only live prepared enough
to finally sit with it.
So I speak into the silence now,
not chasing glory, not applause,

just hoping when my moment comes
I've honoured love's small vows.
That I stayed kind when it was costly,
that I showed up, that I tried
that I leave behind soft memories
instead of wondering why?.

I wish to pass without a crown,
yet leave a tremor in my wake,
to move the world in measured ways
no louder than the risks I take.
If death should call my name one day,
and close the book I couldn't end,
let what I wrote outlive my breath
not as a myth, but till the end.

And if a name must linger softly
when the final page is read,
let "Saar" remain in quiet lines
not louder than the life I led.
No monument, no borrowed light,
just words that learned to stay,
and memories that breathe a little
every time they're read again.

21. शिकवे

" इस किताब की आख़िरी कविता के लिए, मैंने किसी सबसे ख़ूबसूरत एहसास को नहीं चुना।
मैंने उस एहसास को चुना, जो अक्सर सबसे अंत में समझ आता है।
यह कविता रिश्तों की, लम्हों की,
और उन बातों की है, जो रहते हुए साधारण लगती हैं
और छूट जाने के बाद बहुत भारी।
शायद इसलिए यह कविता अंत में होनी ज़रूरी थी, ताकि किताब बंद करते वक़्त
हम थोड़ा रुकें, और आगे बढ़ने से पहले पीछे देख लें।"

भीड़ में जीना सीख लिया हमने,
पर साथ निभाना भूल गए,
जो पास खड़े थे धूप बनकर,
उन्हीं की छाँव से रूठ गए।

हर रोज़ मिला जो साँसों में,
वो सस्ता-सा एहसास लगा,
जो ठहर गया, वही सच निकला,

बाक़ी सब अभ्यास लगा।

रिश्तों को तौलते रहे फ़ायदे में,
नफ़े-नुक़सान की भाषा में,
दिल की कीमत कम आँकी गई,
तालों-चाबियों की आशा में।

जो बोलना था, वो दबता गया,
जो सुनना था, वो छूट गया,
हम जीतते रहे हर बहस में,
और जीवन चुपचाप रूठ गया।

लम्हों की आहट सुनी तक नहीं,
अब उन यादों में खुद को खोते हैं लोग।
जब तक क़रीब थे, शिकवे रहे,
बिछड़ते ही अफ़साने बनाते हैं लोग।

खामोशियों को समझा नहीं,
अब हर ख़त को पढ़कर रोते हैं लोग।
जो धड़कनों में थे, अनसुने रहे,
अब धड़कनों की सदा को खोते हैं लोग।

ये कैसी अजीब सी रस्में यहाँ,
पहले ठुकराते, फिर रोते हैं लोग।
मौजूदगी की क़दर किसी को नहीं...
बाद में तस्वीरें लेकर रोते हैं लोग।

और अंत में "सार" कहता है
जो हाथ में था, वो हाथ न आया,
जो खोया—उसका शोर मचाया।
वक़्त रहते जो अपना न माना,
उसी पर बाद में आँसू बहाया।

Thank You

" Thank you
for staying till the end.
For reading what was written
without explanations,
for feeling what didn't always ask to be understood.
These poems were moments
some fragile, some unfinished.
By reading them,
you gave them meaning.
If even one line stayed with you,
then this book found its reason.
Thank you for being here."

"To the Reader , last tribute"

"You didn't arrive as a reader, you came as a stay,
as breath between lines that had nothing to say.

Where words took a pause, you listened instead,
felt what was written, and what wasn't said.

If these poems were echoes, unsure where to roam,
you became the silence that gave them a home.

So as you turn the last page, quiet and true,
a poem rests easy having been read by you."

www.ingramcontent.com/pod-product-compliance
Lightning Source LLC
Chambersburg PA
CBHW070645240926
51846CB00003BA/789
* 9 7 8 9 3 7 5 1 0 7 5 1 4 *